SUPERHEROES OF SCIENCE

MARY ANNING

FOSSIL HUNTER

Robert Snedden

Gareth Stevens
PUBLISHING

Please visit our website, **www.garethstevens.com**. For a free color catalog of all our high-quality books, call toll free 1-800-542-2595 or fax 1-877-542-2596.

Library of Congress Cataloging-in-Publication Data

Snedden, Robert.
Mary Anning: fossil hunter / by Robert Snedden.
p. cm. – (Superheroes of science)
Includes index.
ISBN 978-1-4824-3145-2 (pbk.)
ISBN 978-1-4824-3148-3 (6 pack)
ISBN 978-1-4824-3146-9 (library binding)
1. Anning, Mary, – 1799-1847 – Juvenile literature. 2. Anning, Mary, – 1799-1847 – Childhood and youth – Juvenile literature. 3. Women paleontologists – England – Biography – Juvenile literature.
I. Snedden, Robert. II. Title.
QE707.A56 D53 2016
560'.92–d23

First Edition

Published in 2016 by
Gareth Stevens Publishing
111 East 14th Street, Suite 349
New York, NY 10003

© 2016 Gareth Stevens Publishing

Produced for Gareth Stevens by Calcium
Editors for Calcium: 3REDCARS
Designers: Paul Myerscough and 3REDCARS

Picture credits: Cover art by Mat Edwards; Dreamstime: Baloncici 33c, Bidouze Stéphane 22t, Nahuel Condino 23b, Sergey Lavrentev 29b, Michelle Pustejovsky 26c, Steveheap 20c, Velazquez77 19t, Martin Žák 45t; Shutterstock: Andy Fox Photography 9c, Balefire 13b, Jon Bilous 15t, 501room 4b, Martin Kemp 42t, MarcelClemens 38t, MichaelTaylor3d 21c, Nicku 44t, Number001 10b, Lefteris Papaulakis 42c, Dr. Morley Read 8b, Michael Rosskothen 13t, Denis Rozhnovsky 7t, Sombra 18c, Tupungato 40t, Kristina Vackova 28t, Wollertz 31c, Yu Lan 10t; Wikimedia Commons: 16t, 25c, 27b, 34c, 35c, 37t, Ballista 41c, Biographies of Scientific Men 36b, William Buckland 24c, B.J. Donne 5c, Gaius Cornelius 6c, Henry De la Beche 32b, Jean-Henri Marlet 17b, "Martin" 39c, Poozeum 30b, Royal Society 14c.

Printed in the United States of America

CPSIA compliance information: Batch #CS15GS: For further information contact Gareth Stevens, New York, New York at 1-800-542-2595.

CONTENTS

Chapter 1
THE GREATEST FOSSIL HUNTER

The Natural History Museum in London, England, has called Mary Anning the greatest fossil hunter ever known. She discovered fossils–plants and creatures preserved in rock for millions of years–that shook up the way we look at the natural world and how it has changed over time. Her achievements inspired many scientists and paved the way for the development of geology as a science.

When Anning lived, around two centuries ago, people were beginning to rethink their ideas about how the world had come to be the way it is, and there was growing interest in geology, the science of Earth. Geologists look at the materials that Earth is made of and how they are formed. These scientists are interested in the history of our planet,

Kpow!

Mary Anning became famous for her spectacular fossil finds, like this ichthyosaur.

4

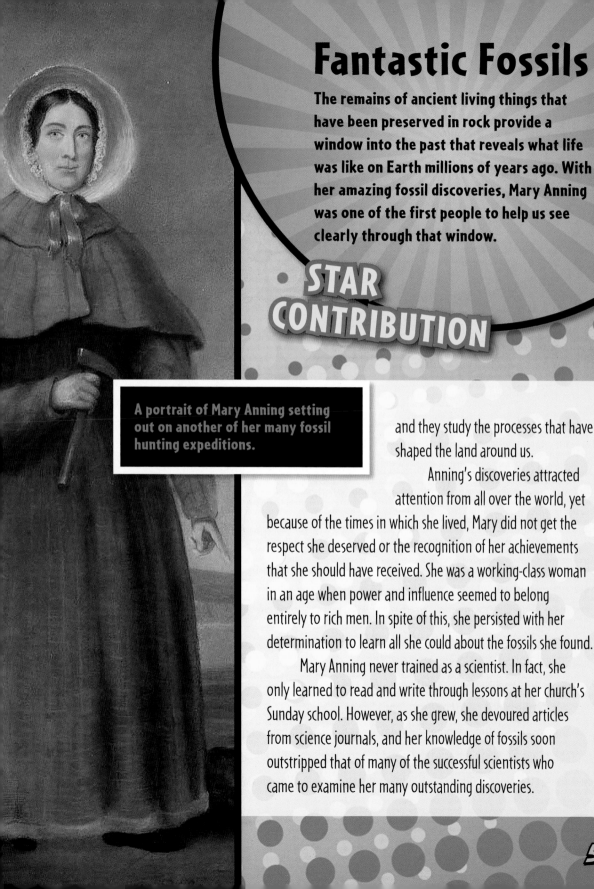

Fantastic Fossils

The remains of ancient living things that have been preserved in rock provide a window into the past that reveals what life was like on Earth millions of years ago. With her amazing fossil discoveries, Mary Anning was one of the first people to help us see clearly through that window.

STAR CONTRIBUTION

A portrait of Mary Anning setting out on another of her many fossil hunting expeditions.

and they study the processes that have shaped the land around us.

Anning's discoveries attracted attention from all over the world, yet because of the times in which she lived, Mary did not get the respect she deserved or the recognition of her achievements that she should have received. She was a working-class woman in an age when power and influence seemed to belong entirely to rich men. In spite of this, she persisted with her determination to learn all she could about the fossils she found.

Mary Anning never trained as a scientist. In fact, she only learned to read and write through lessons at her church's Sunday school. However, as she grew, she devoured articles from science journals, and her knowledge of fossils soon outstripped that of many of the successful scientists who came to examine her many outstanding discoveries.

MIRACULOUS ESCAPE

Mary Anning was born May 21, 1799, in the town of Lyme Regis, on the south coast of England. Her parents were Richard and Mary Anning. Childhood diseases, such as measles, were common at the time and often fatal. Of the Annings's ten children, only Mary and her older brother Joseph survived into adulthood.

Living close to the sea was also a danger. The family's home was built on a bridge and sometimes flooded in bad weather. On one occasion the family had to crawl out of an upstairs window to avoid drowning.

Little Mary was only one year old when she had an extraordinarily close escape from death. On August 19, 1800, her nurse Elizabeth Haskin had taken her out for the day. A sudden storm sent Elizabeth running for the shelter of some elm trees. There, a flash of lightning left Elizabeth and two other women dead. By some miracle, Mary was found alive and returned unharmed to her relieved mother. According to local legend, it was the lightning that made Mary such a bright and lively child.

MARY ANNING
1799 - 1847

The famous fossilist was born here in a house on the site of Lyme Regis Museum. The house was her home & her fossil shop until 1826

More about Mary Anning inside the Museum

Mary Anning's house and shop drawn in 1842. It was demolished in 1889 to make way for the museum

A special plaque commemorates Mary Anning's birthplace and first fossil store in Lyme Regis.

Celebrating Mary

Lyme Regis still holds an annual Mary Anning Day, with events to celebrate her birthday, and also an annual Fossil Festival. Its museum has exhibitions about her discoveries and organizes guided walks around the town so that people can see where Mary lived and worked.

SUPERHERO FACT

A bolt of lightning came close to ending Mary Anning's life when it had just begun.

Smart or not, Mary had little chance of education as a child but was able to attend a Congregationalist Sunday school. The Congregationalists believed that poor people should be educated, and Mary learned to read and write. One of her treasured possessions was a copy of the *Dissenters' Theological Magazine and Review*. It included one essay by her church's pastor that described how God created the world in six days and another in which he encouraged Congregationalists to take up the study of geology.

Mary's father also inspired her interest in fossils but was criticized by his fellow Congregationalists for going out hunting for fossils on holy days, such as Good Friday. People were also worried when he started to take his children with him as many thought it was far too dangerous for them out on the cliffs.

BATTERED BY THE SEA

Lyme Regis lies in Lyme Bay, on the coast of the English Channel that separates England from France. Today, it is a small town with a population of fewer than 4,000 people. For centuries before Mary Anning's birth, it had been an important port. The townspeople were proud of the Cobb–a breakwater 600 feet (183 m) long that had been built to shelter ships from storms and high seas. However, at the time when Mary was born, the ships were growing too big for Lyme Regis's shallow waters, and trade was moving to larger ports.

The beaches and cliffs around the town form part of the Jurassic Coast, now a World Heritage Site. The area is famous for the fossil finds that have been made there. Pounding waves and storms cause

Wow!

Fossil ammonites like this are common along the shores of Lyme Regis where Mary lived.

Epic Shores

The Jurassic Coast, which is 95 miles (153 km) long, is the only place on Earth where 185 million years of our planet's history have been exposed to view. Walking east along the coast is like taking a walk through time from 250 million to 65 million years ago. Mary Anning only ever saw a small part of it, as she never went more than walking distance from her home in Lyme Regis.

SUPERHERO STAT

The Jurassic Coast in winter could be a cold and dangerous place to hunt for fossils.

frequent landslides along the fragile cliffs, often revealing a fresh crop of fossils.

Traveling from west to east along the Jurassic Coast, the rocks are generally laid out from oldest to youngest. Usually these layers of rock would have formed one on top of the other, and the oldest rocks would be hidden from sight by the newer ones. However, around 100 million years ago movements in Earth tilted the rocks to the east. The exposed rocks in the west were gradually eroded, revealing the ancient layers that had been buried for millions of years. Over time, erosion gradually created the coast that can be seen today–the cliffs exposing the layers of rock to view.

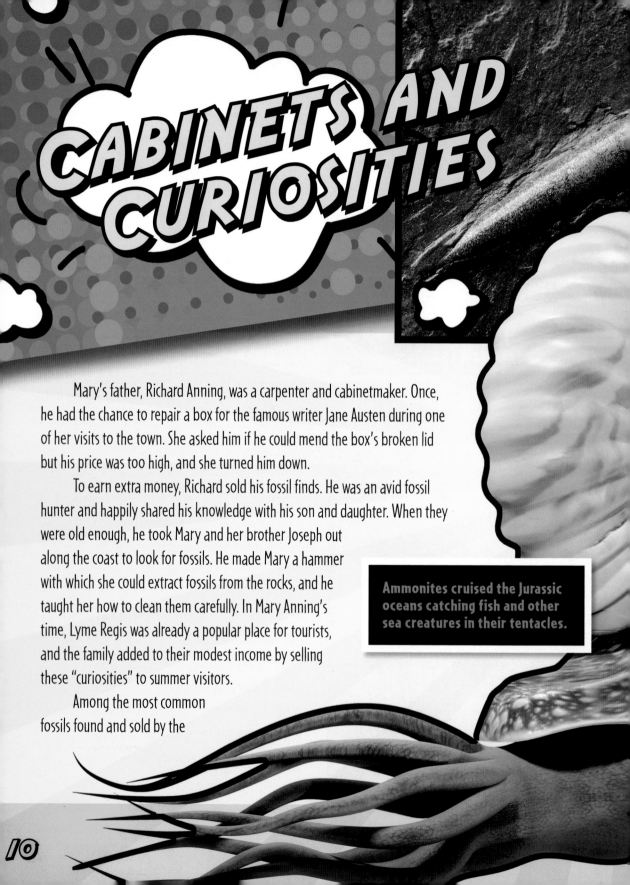

CABINETS AND CURIOSITIES

Mary's father, Richard Anning, was a carpenter and cabinetmaker. Once, he had the chance to repair a box for the famous writer Jane Austen during one of her visits to the town. She asked him if he could mend the box's broken lid but his price was too high, and she turned him down.

To earn extra money, Richard sold his fossil finds. He was an avid fossil hunter and happily shared his knowledge with his son and daughter. When they were old enough, he took Mary and her brother Joseph out along the coast to look for fossils. He made Mary a hammer with which she could extract fossils from the rocks, and he taught her how to clean them carefully. In Mary Anning's time, Lyme Regis was already a popular place for tourists, and the family added to their modest income by selling these "curiosities" to summer visitors.

Among the most common fossils found and sold by the

Ammonites cruised the Jurassic oceans catching fish and other sea creatures in their tentacles.

She Sells Seashells

The Annings' fossil stall in Lyme Regis was so popular that some people believe that Mary was the inspiration for the well-known tongue twister, "She sells seashells by the seashore."

The hard inner shell of the belemnite is usually the only part of the creature that forms a fossil.

Annings were ammonites. These beautiful spiral shells, ranging in size from a few inches to more than 6 feet (2 m) across, were the remains of creatures that swam in Earth's ancient oceans around 240 million to 65 million years ago. The Annings also sold belemnites–conical-shaped fossils that were the internal shells of sea animals that lived around the same time as the ammonites and were related to today's octopuses and squid. These fossils were sometimes called "thunderbolts" because it was once believed that they were created by lightning strikes.

The Annings were not the only fossil hunters in Lyme Regis. The Philpot sisters were also well known as collectors. One of the sisters, Elizabeth, made friends with Mary, even though she was nearly 20 years older. The two were soon going on fossil expeditions together, and Elizabeth encouraged Mary to learn all she could about the fossils she discovered and the rocks she found them in.

Chapter 2

DEATH AND DISCOVERY

Winter was the best time for making new fossil discoveries as the high winds and rain brought fresh parts of the cliffs tumbling down. However, the winter weather also made conditions on the cliffs tricky and dangerous.

In the winter of 1809–10, Richard Anning had a terrible accident while walking the cliff paths to Charmouth, near Lyme Regis. He slipped and fell from the boggy slopes of the Black Ven cliff. Weakened by his injuries, he later contracted tuberculosis, a disease of the lungs. On October 15, 1810, at just 44 years old, Richard died from a combination of illness and injury. His family was left poor and in debt.

SUPERHERO FACT

Valuable Find

According to one story, not long after her father's death, ten-year-old Mary went down to the beach to look for fossils. She found an ammonite and was carrying it home when a woman in the street stopped her and offered her half a crown (about $10 today) for it. Mary was delighted and handed over the ammonite. From that moment she was determined to be a fossil hunter.

Landslides such as this one on Charmouth Beach made life hazardous for the fossil hunter.

Bash!

Mary Anning would have used a hammer very similar to this to remove fossils from the rocks.

Mary was nearly 11 years old and her brother 15 when their father died. The Anning family suffered great hardship and had to depend on charity to survive. Hoping to earn some money from their finds, they determined to continue their fossil trade. Although still young, Mary and her brother had learned enough from their father to carry on collecting fossils by themselves.

Mary's mother ran the business side of things and encouraged her increasingly knowledgeable children where she could. She was also a skilled fossil collector and had often gone with her husband on his fossil-hunting expeditions. By the time of his death, Richard had also built up a good reputation for his fossil finds. In 1810, one collector wrote to his friend, "There is a person at Lyme who collects for sale by the name of Anning ... I would advise you calling upon him."

GIANT FISH LIZARD!

Blam!

Soon after his father's death, Joseph Anning found a skull protruding from a cliff. At first, he thought it was that of a crocodile. The skull was about 4 feet (1.2 m) long and was narrow with eye sockets like saucers.

In 1812, Mary returned and uncovered much more of the skeleton–including fossilized neck bones, 60 vertebrae, and ribs. The creature was later identified as an ichthyosaur, which means, "fish lizard." It is not known exactly where, but the fossil was probably found to the east of Lyme Regis, near the foot of the Church Cliffs, part of the oldest rock formation along the Jurassic Coast.

Ichthyosaurs swam in the ocean between 250 and 90 million years ago. Despite the name, they were neither fish nor lizards. They were air-breathing reptiles, so they would have to come to the surface regularly for air, just as whales and dolphins do in today's oceans. Rather than laying eggs, the females gave birth to live young ichthyosaurs.

Mary's Great Ichthyosaur

Partial remains of ichthyosaurs had first been found more than 100 years before the Annings' discoveries. However, this was the first time an almost complete skeleton had been uncovered. It gave scientists a chance to develop ideas about how the ichthyosaur from long ago had lived.

STAR CONTRIBUTION

It is likely that they propelled themselves through the water by flicking their powerful tails and used their flippers for steering. The ichthyosaurs would have cruised the waters hunting fish, squid, and other ocean creatures. Their huge eye sockets suggest that they hunted deep beneath the ocean surface where light levels are low.

The strange creature caught the popular imagination of Mary's time. A Scottish academic, Professor John Stuart Blackie of Edinburgh, even wrote about it in his poem "A Song of Geology":

Behold, a strange monster our wonder engages.
If dolphin or lizard your wit may defy.
Some thirty feet long on the shore of Lyme-Regis
With a saw for a jaw, and a big staring eye.

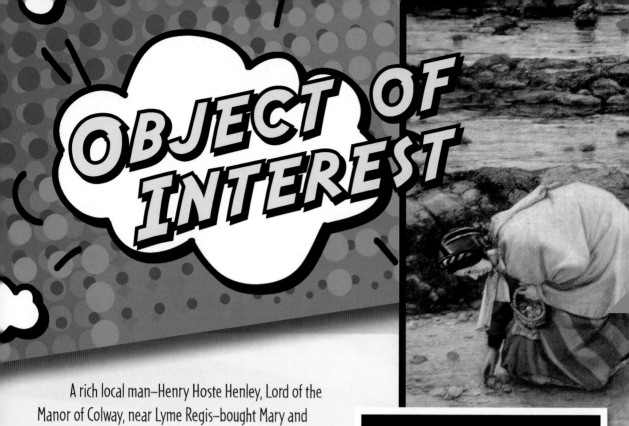

OBJECT OF INTEREST

A rich local man–Henry Hoste Henley, Lord of the Manor of Colway, near Lyme Regis–bought Mary and Joseph's ichthyosaur. Henley owned large parts of Lyme Regis, including the beach and the cliffs where the fossil was found. He paid the family about £23 (around $1,000 today) for the skeleton.

Henley sold the fossil to the collector William Bullock who displayed it in his Museum of Natural Curiosities in London, where it attracted great interest. In 1819, the fossil was bought by the British Museum for £45 (worth about $2,000 today). The skull and neck are still on display today in London's Natural History Museum.

In 1814, Sir Everard Home, a well-known English surgeon, wrote the first scientific description of the ichthyosaur. As was to happen so often in her life, Mary Anning was never mentioned as the collector of the fossil. Home even gave credit for its cleaning and preparation to the staff at William Bullock's museum, though it was actually Mary who had carried out this painstaking task. Home could not make up his mind about what sort of creature the ichthyosaur was. At one time he thought it was a fish, then perhaps a relative of the duck-billed platypus, or a cross between a salamander and a lizard.

Groundbreaking New Science

In the early nineteenth century, most people still believed that the world was just a few thousand years old. Mary Anning's discoveries were groundbreaking. The fossil evidence which she did so much to uncover and bring to the attention of science, raised new questions about the development of life. It revealed how different the creatures that had inhabited Earth in the distant past were from those of today.

STAR CONTRIBUTION

Between 1815 and 1819, Mary Anning went on to find several more ichthyosaur fossils. In 1821, William Conybeare and Henry De La Beche of the Geological Society of London made a study of the ichthyosaur specimens. They decided that ichthyosaurs were a type of marine reptile, previously unknown to science.

William Bullock was an avid collector of natural history objects, including fossils.

Chapter 3
SPECTACULAR FOSSIL FINDS

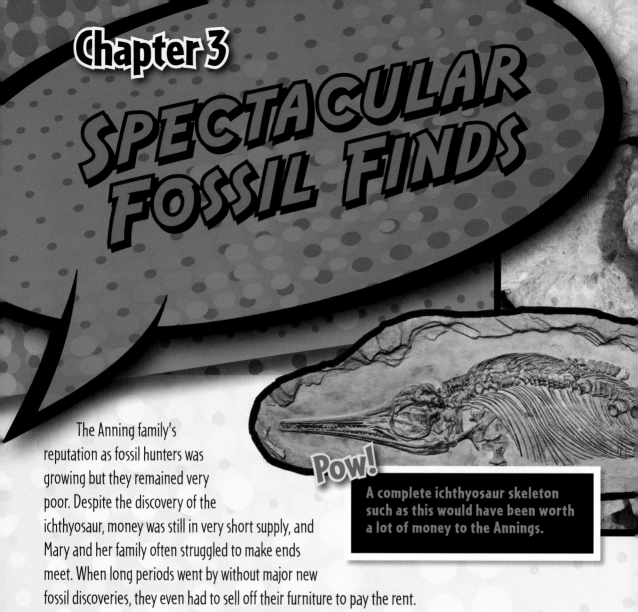

Pow!

A complete ichthyosaur skeleton such as this would have been worth a lot of money to the Annings.

The Anning family's reputation as fossil hunters was growing but they remained very poor. Despite the discovery of the ichthyosaur, money was still in very short supply, and Mary and her family often struggled to make ends meet. When long periods went by without major new fossil discoveries, they even had to sell off their furniture to pay the rent.

Most of the fossils the Annings were selling were ammonites and belemnites, which were fairly common and so could not be sold for a high price. An ichthyosaur skeleton was worth much more money, but this kind of fossil was much rarer and harder to find.

One of the family's customers was Lieutenant-Colonel Thomas James Birch, an avid fossil collector and a regular visitor to nearby Charmouth. He heard about the Annings' circumstances and thought that they should not be living in such "considerable difficulty." He decided to do something about their financial situation.

Mary Takes Charge

By the middle of the 1820s, Mary had increasingly taken over the running of the business from her mother. Her brother Joseph was also becoming less involved in the finding and selling of fossils, as he had taken up an apprenticeship with an upholsterer. By 1825, he had given up fossil hunting altogether.

Because they were so common, only the very best ammonite fossils brought a good price.

In 1820, Birch held an auction to sell off his fossil collection. He wrote to say that the sale was "for the benefit of the poor woman, and her son and daughter at Lyme, who have in truth found almost all the fine things which have been submitted to scientific investigation." Many of the specimens he sold were ones he had already bought from the Annings.

The sale attracted interest from fossil collectors all over Europe and raised £400 (more than $40,000 in today's money). Lieutenant-Colonel Birch handed over much of the proceeds—although no one is sure quite how much—to the Anning family. The publicity from the auction also helped to spread Mary Anning's fame and establish her standing as an exceptional fossil collector.

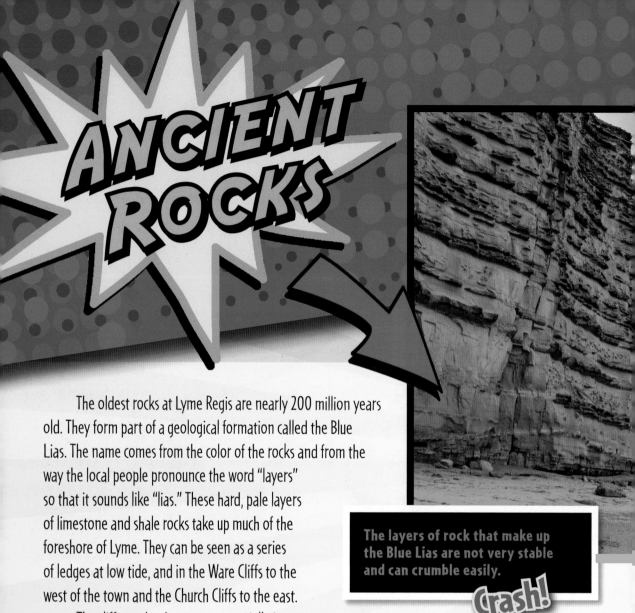

ANCIENT ROCKS

The oldest rocks at Lyme Regis are nearly 200 million years old. They form part of a geological formation called the Blue Lias. The name comes from the color of the rocks and from the way the local people pronounce the word "layers" so that it sounds like "lias." These hard, pale layers of limestone and shale rocks take up much of the foreshore of Lyme. They can be seen as a series of ledges at low tide, and in the Ware Cliffs to the west of the town and the Church Cliffs to the east.

The layers of rock that make up the Blue Lias are not very stable and can crumble easily.

Crash!

The cliffs can be dangerous, especially in winter, when the rain can cause landslides. Richard Anning found this out to his cost. The Black Ven where he fell lies just above the Church Cliffs.

The layers that make up the Blue Lias were laid down on an ancient seabed 200 to 195 million years ago, during the Jurassic Period. This area was once beneath the sea, which explains why few fossils of land-living dinosaurs are found at Lyme Regis. The waters must have been rich in marine animals, such as fish, ammonites, belemnites,

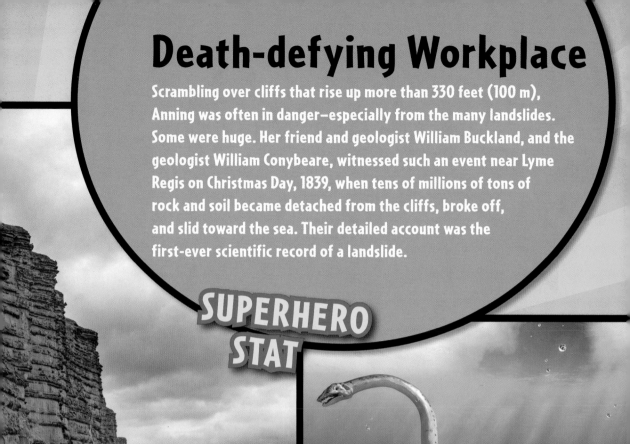

Death-defying Workplace

Scrambling over cliffs that rise up more than 330 feet (100 m), Anning was often in danger—especially from the many landslides. Some were huge. Her friend and geologist William Buckland, and the geologist William Conybeare, witnessed such an event near Lyme Regis on Christmas Day, 1839, when tens of millions of tons of rock and soil became detached from the cliffs, broke off, and slid toward the sea. Their detailed account was the first-ever scientific record of a landslide.

SUPERHERO STAT

Among Mary's fossil finds were plesiosaurs. These were large creatures that could reach 65 feet (20 m) in length.

plesiosaurs, and ichthyosaurs, judging by the abundance of fossils that have been found.

As the Annings well knew, the Blue Lias cliffs are a fine source of good ammonite fossils. A visitor to Lyme Regis today can see the ammonite graveyard, to the west of the town, at Monmouth Beach, below the Ware Cliffs. Hundreds of large ammonites—some more than 3 feet (1 m) across—have been exposed in the rock among the boulders on the beach.

A WINDOW ON THE PAST

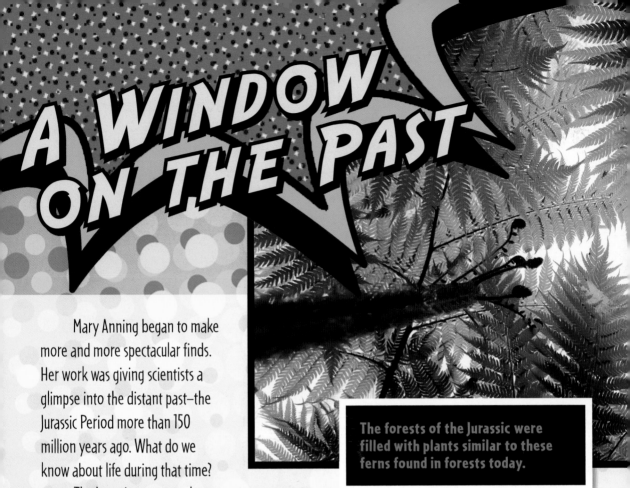

Mary Anning began to make more and more spectacular finds. Her work was giving scientists a glimpse into the distant past—the Jurassic Period more than 150 million years ago. What do we know about life during that time?

The forests of the Jurassic were filled with plants similar to these ferns found in forests today.

The Jurassic was named from the Jura Mountains, bordering France and Switzerland, where rocks from this period were first studied. It spanned around 55 million years of Earth's history from around 200 million to 145 million years ago. There was an abundance of plant life in the Jurassic, but there were no flowering plants. It would be another 50 million years or so before the first flowers appeared. The landscape was dominated by ferns, ginkgoes, palm-like cycads, and conifers—including ancestors of today's redwoods and pine trees.

It was a time when giant plant-eating dinosaurs, such as *Diplodocus* and *Brachiosaurus*, the largest animals ever to wander Earth's surface, roamed across the landscape feasting on the greenery. Alongside them were other plant eaters, such as *Stegosaurus*, with impressive bony plates running along its back. There were also fearsome predators, such as the fast-moving *Velociraptor* and the formidable *Allosaurus*, which was 32 feet (10 m) long. The mighty pterosaurs, some with wingspans

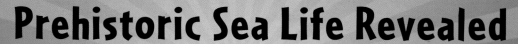

Prehistoric Sea Life Revealed

In the sea that covered most of Britain and Europe in the Jurassic Period were great ichthyosaurs and long-necked plesiosaurs. Anning brought their remains to light millions of years after they vanished from the living world. There were fish, too, and ancient relatives of the squid and octopuses found in today's oceans. These included the belemnites and ammonites, whose fossilized shells the Annings and other fossil hunters uncovered and sold.

STAR CONTRIBUTION

of 50 feet (15 m), flew in the skies above. The first birds, such as *Archaeopteryx*, also appeared at this time.

Lurking in the undergrowth of the Jurassic forests, trying to avoid being eaten, were the first warm-blooded mammals. Most of them were no bigger than rats. Millions of years later, they would evolve into the animals we are so familiar with today, such as sheep, lions, giraffes, wolves, and–of course–us.

The fast-moving *Velociraptors* were among the deadliest predators of the Jurassic Period.

Zoom!

DISCOVERY AND EXTINCTION

In 1823, Anning found a complete skeleton of the long-necked plesiosaurus. Like the ichthyosaurs, the plesiosaurs were air-breathing reptiles, adapted for life in the water. They had short tails, broad, flat bodies, flippers for swimming, and long slender necks.

Plesiosaur remains had been known for more than 200 years. In 1821, the geologists William Conybeare and Henry De La Beche had examined a partial skeleton from Lieutenant-Colonel Birch's collection and realized that it represented a completely new type of animal. They named it *Plesiosaurus*. Anning had found the partial skeleton, but Conybeare did not mention that. He reported the finding to a meeting of the Geological Society in 1824. Even though he used Anning's sketch of the plesiosaur in his presentation, he once again neglected to mention that she was the collector.

Kpow!

The plesiosaur skeleton found in 1823 by Mary Anning was sketched by her friend William Buckland.

The famous French anatomist Georges Cuvier thought at first that the plesiosaur was a fake. Once he realized that the reptile was in fact genuine, his approval gave a great boost to Anning's reputation as an exceptional fossil hunter.

Fishy Find

In 1829, Anning discovered the fossil remains of a previously unknown fish called *Squaloraja polyspondyla* in the Blue Lias rocks. It had features that were similar to those of a shark and a ray and appeared to be a link between the two types of fish.

STAR CONTRIBUTION

Cuvier was the world's leading expert on the anatomy of animals. He used his knowledge to explain fossils with great insight. The story has it that—from just a few fragments of bones—Cuvier could describe what a previously unknown animal had looked like with amazing accuracy.

After studying elephant fossils found near Paris, Cuvier discovered that their bones were different from those of living elephants in Africa and India. He decided that they must be an entirely different type of elephant that had vanished, or become extinct. For many people in Mary Anning's day, the idea of extinction was distinctly troubling. If God had created all of nature at the beginning of the world, it seemed unlikely that some parts of that creation would be allowed to die off and disappear.

The Frenchman Georges Cuvier was one of the founders of the new science of paleontology.

Chapter 4

FOSSIL DEPOT AND BEYOND!

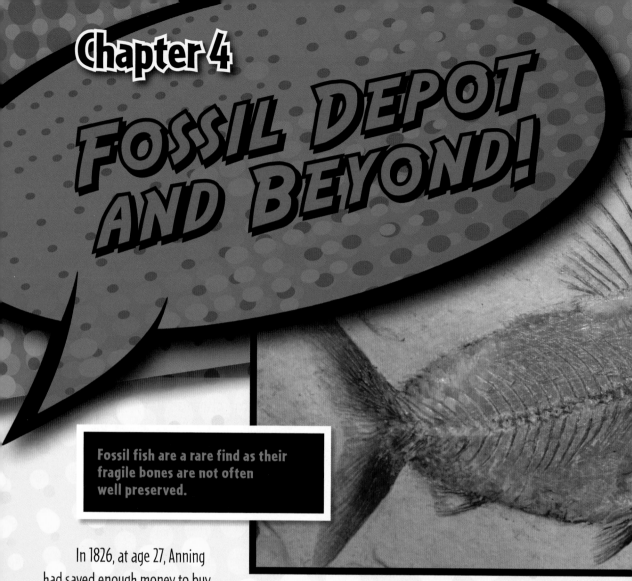

Fossil fish are a rare find as their fragile bones are not often well preserved.

In 1826, at age 27, Anning had saved enough money to buy a home with a large front window. Here, she opened her shop, "Anning's Fossil Depot," an event that was reported in the local newspaper. A simple white sign outside was all that drew attention to the shop.

Many geologists and fossil collectors from all over Europe and the United States came to visit the Fossil Depot. One of those was George William Featherstonhaugh who, in 1834, was appointed the first United States government geologist. Apparently he thought Anning "a very clever, funny creature." When he visited the Fossil Depot in 1827, he bought fossils for the New York Lyceum of Natural History (now the New York Academy of Sciences).

A Royal Visitor

In 1844, toward the end of Anning's life, another visitor to the Fossil Depot was King Frederick Augustus of Saxony. He bought an ichthyosaur skeleton to add to his collection. The king's doctor, who went with him, wrote, "We fell in with a shop in which the most remarkable fossil remains ... were exhibited in the window." He thought the price of £15 (almost $2,000 today) that Anning asked for the ichthyosaur was "very moderate." When the doctor asked Anning to write her name and address in his pocketbook for future reference, she told him, "I am well known throughout the whole of Europe."

SUPERHERO FACT

In 1834, the Swiss-born biologist and geologist Louis Agassiz visited Anning. Agassiz would be the first to suggest that Earth had been frozen by an ice age and that the ice age shaped much of the landscape, and not the flood of Noah, as many believed.

Agassiz was the only person to name a species after her during her lifetime. Though she was by this time well known around the world for the importance of her finds, she continued to struggle for recognition for her work. In the early 1840s, Agassiz named two fossil fish after her—*Acrodus anningiae* and *Belenostomus anningiae*—and named another after Anning's fellow fossil hunter, Elizabeth Philpot. Agassiz was grateful for the help the women had given him in finding fossil fish and thanked them in his book *Studies of Fossil Fish*.

Louis Agassiz was a highly respected researcher. He became professor of zoology at Harvard University.

STEEP LEARNING CURVE

Mary Anning's formal education had been limited, but this did not stop her from reading as much scientific literature as she could lay her hands on. For Anning, hunting for fossils was not just a way of earning a living. It opened up a whole world of learning for her.

The cuttlefish of today is one of the closest living relatives of the now-extinct belemnites.

Whoosh!

She taught herself geology, paleontology, anatomy, and scientific illustration. She would often copy scientific papers by hand, even making copies of detailed technical drawings, which were so accurate that it was hard to tell her drawings apart from the originals.

Many of the people Mary was dealing with were well-educated men of science. Her surviving letters are proof that she could share ideas with them with great confidence. Many of the scientists were impressed by her knowledge of anatomy, and she was not afraid to argue with them if she thought their ideas were mistaken. There were others, though, who refused to believe that an uneducated young woman like Anning could have such knowledge and skill.

In 1826, Anning discovered what appeared to be a chamber containing dried ink inside a belemnite fossil. She saw at once how closely the fossilized ink chamber resembled the ink sacs of modern-day squid and cuttlefish.

Inside Investigator

Anning did not simply collect fossils. She also dissected animals, such as fish and cuttlefish, so that she could compare their anatomy with that of their earlier fossil relatives. This helped her gain a better understanding of the fossils she discovered, and later helped other fossil hunters and scientists to understand the anatomy of prehistoric creatures and relate them to the animals we know today.

STAR CONTRIBUTION

It must have been quite exciting to write with ink found inside the remains of a belemnite that died millions of years ago.

She showed the fossil ink chamber to her friend Elizabeth Philpot. Philpot found that by grinding up the dried ink and mixing it with water it could readily be used for writing and sketching. Soon local artists were making use of the fossilized belemnite ink chambers as a free source of ink. Anning's discovery of the ink chambers led William Buckland, who lectured in geology at the University of Oxford, to conclude that the belemnites had used ink for defense, just as cuttlefish and octopuses do today.

DRAGONS AND DROPPINGS

In 1828, Anning discovered a "flying dragon." William Buckland described it as "a monster, resembling nothing that had been seen or heard upon the Earth." Its body and legs were like those of a lizard, but it had wings and claws like a bat and a long beak full of teeth.

Mary's discovery, however, was not a dragon but a pterosaur. She was probably very puzzled by her find, as it was unlike anything else she had seen previously. The pterosaurs were flying reptiles that lived between about 225 million and 65 million years ago. Their hollow bones made them light enough to fly, and they had large wings of skin that stretched from long fingers to their bodies. The pterosaurs probably lived on land but may have flown out over the sea to catch fish. Pterosaurs were not dinosaurs but were likely close relatives.

Buckland often visited Lyme and frequently went fossil hunting with Anning. She had

Yuk!

Coprolites may not look glamorous but they are important to our understanding of prehistoric life.

Really Rare Find

Pterosaurs are rare fossils. Anning's was the first to be found in Britain and only the third in the world. The type she found, called *Dimorphodon*, is particularly rare. Since 1828, only one other specimen with a skull has been found of this animal.

SUPERHERO FACT

Because pterosaur bones are lightweight and fragile they do not form fossils easily.

noticed that some odd cone-shaped fossils, called bezoar stones, were sometimes found inside the abdomens of ichthyosaurs. She had also discovered that, if the bezoar stones were broken open, fossilized fish bones, and sometimes even small ichthyosaur bones, were revealed inside.

Anning believed that the stones were actually fossilized feces and suggested this to Buckland. Her suggestion turned out to be true. Examining the bezoar stones would give valuable insights into the diets of these long-extinct creatures. After more investigation, Buckland published his findings in 1829, giving the stones the name "coprolites." When Buckland presented his findings on coprolites to the Geological Society, he actually mentioned Anning by name and praised her skill in uncovering the truth about the bezoar stones. It was one of the few times she was properly credited.

Chapter 5

A WOMAN IN A MAN'S WORLD

GEOLOGICAL

Through her own efforts, Mary Anning knew more about fossils than did many of the wealthy collectors who bought them from her. However, it was men who published details of her findings, and they often neglected even to give her a mention. Most of Anning's finds ended up in museums and personal collections—without any credit given to her as the person who had actually discovered the fossils. Understandably, she resented these slights.

The Geological Society of London refused to allow women members and did not even let women attend meetings as guests. The "gentleman geologists" of the society met regularly to discuss the latest findings. Anning was excluded from these discussions. It was not until 1904 that the society actually allowed women members. Anning was eventually made an honorary member after her death. Geologist Hugh

A sketch by her friend Henry De la Beche shows Mary Anning fossil hunting on a Dorset cliff.

Star Note-taker

The ending of one letter about her finds, addressed to Johann Samuel Miller, curator of the Bristol Institution for the Advancement of Science and Art, reveals the extreme care Anning took to record her findings. She was writing to compare a ray fish she had dissected with a fossil fish she had found on the rocks on the shore, noting their differing backbones. "The tide warns me I must leave off scribbling," she ended it, suggesting she was taking notes of the fossil on the beach as she wrote. Careful note-taking is an essential part of good science.

SUPERHERO FACT

Torrens, writing in 1992, spoke of how those who bought Anning's fossils had been honored, while she "as workman and tradesman, is invisible."

The fact that Anning was both working class and a woman meant that her contributions to the new science of paleontology were often overlooked. However, she did get some recognition for her talents. In 1824, Lady Harriet Silvester, the widow of an important London lawyer, wrote in her diary after visiting Anning, "... the extraordinary thing in this young woman is that she has made herself so thoroughly acquainted with the science, that the moment she finds any bones, she knows to what tribe they belong ... by reading and application she has arrived to that degree of knowledge as to be in the habit of writing and talking with professors and other clever men on the subject, and they all acknowledge that she understands more of the science than anyone else in this kingdom."

The door to the Geological Society in London remained closed to women until 1904.

SECOND-RATE STATUS

In Anning's time, women were ranked lower than men in nearly all aspects of life. They were not allowed to vote, to hold public office, or to attend university.

British society of the day was divided rigidly into different classes. There were few careers for working-class women beyond domestic service, factory labor, or work on farms. Women from the middle classes had even fewer choices, with little beyond teaching or being a companion to a wealthier lady. When she got married, a woman signed over all her rights to her husband. He controlled any property and money she had, including any earnings.

The highly independent Anning never married—at a time when most women were married before their twenties. The English paleontologist Gideon Mantell described her as, "a prim, pedantic, vinegar-looking, thin female, shrewd and rather satirical in her conversation." Mary was probably a match for most of the men she came

Gideon Mantell was credited with discovering four of the five different types of dinosaur known at the time of his death.

Women Go for Geology

Anning is a wonderful role model but was not the only female contributing to the new science of geology. William Buckland's wife, Mary, often helped him collect specimens, as did Mary Ann Mantell, wife of Gideon Mantell. Mary Buckland even had her own fossil collection. These women also made sketches of specimens, and helped their husbands to prepare and write their papers. In fact, it was Mary Mantell who found the teeth of the dinosaur *Iguanodon*, which led to her husband's paper announcing the discovery of this new giant reptile.

STAR CONTRIBUTION

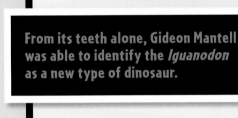

From its teeth alone, Gideon Mantell was able to identify the *Iguanodon* as a new type of dinosaur.

Snap!

across. She is said to have called the men of Lyme, "things or numbskulls, not men."

A woman alone in the company of men could also cause local gossip. Mary sometimes went fossil hunting with William Buckland, which did not go unnoticed in the town. As Buckland's daughter noted in her biography of him, "For years afterwards, local gossip preserved traditions of his adventures with that geological celebrity, Mary Anning, in whose company he was to be seen wading up to his knees in search of fossils." Anning probably paid no attention to such rumors and certainly remained friendly with Buckland's children when he moved his family to Lyme Regis.

HARDSHIP AND HELP

In 1830, the economy in Britain was on a downturn, and the sales of fossils fell. Anning once again struggled to make ends meet.

However, her geologist friend Henry De La Beche helped her out. He had prints made of his own watercolor painting of life in prehistoric Dorset, which was based on fossils Anning had found. De La Beche sold copies of the print to his wealthy friends and donated the proceeds to Anning.

Around this time, Anning decided to leave the local Congregational church, which she and her family had always attended, and where she had been baptized and learned to read and write. Instead she became a member of the Anglican Church. A devout Christian, who almost never missed Sunday service, Anning remained as active in her new church as she had been in her old one.

While changing churches was partly prompted by the arrival of a

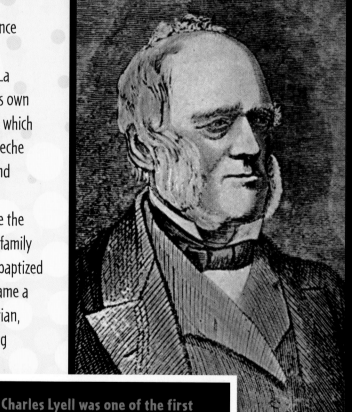

Charles Lyell was one of the first to describe the processes that had formed Earth over billions of years.

Fossil Funds

In December 1830, after a long period without any major finds, Anning discovered the skeleton of a new type of plesiosaur. She sold it for £200 (about $25,000 today)—more than a year's income for many people at that time. It must have been a very welcome addition to her earnings.

SUPERHERO STAT

Henry De la Beche fired imaginations with his illustrations of how life in the Jurassic might have looked.

Kpow!

new unpopular pastor, it may also have been a bid by Anning to gain greater respectability. The gentleman geologists with whom she dealt included ordained clergy such as William Buckland and William Conybeare.

One of Anning's correspondents was the Scottish geologist Charles Lyell. He had been a student at the University of Oxford and attended many of Buckland's lectures on geology. Lyell wrote to Anning asking about the effect the sea was having on the coast at Lyme Regis. In 1830, he published the first part of his *Principles of Geology*. This book made his reputation as one of the greatest geologists of the century. In it he set out his reasons for believing that the surface of Earth had been formed by slow processes, taking place over a long time.

Chapter 6

NEW WORLD OF IDEAS

Our world has existed for 4.6 billion years and has undergone many changes in that time.

Until the 1820s, many scientists simply did not believe that new species could appear or that existing ones could become extinct. Most people thought that the world was only a few thousand years old. Geologists, such as Charles Lyell, were challenging these beliefs and suggesting that Earth was hundreds of millions of years old. Scientists today have calculated that our planet was formed around 4.6 billion years ago—making it much older than even Lyell imagined.

Any fossil discoveries that differed from known living creatures were at that time explained as representing animals that must still live somewhere in some—as yet unexplored—area of the world. However, some of Anning's discoveries were so unlike any living species that this idea was hard to sustain.

There were many attempts to use stories from the Bible to explain the new fossil discoveries. For example, Anning's friend William Buckland believed that the fossils found at high altitudes proved that a great flood, like Noah's flood described in the Bible, had once covered the planet.

Monsters from the Dark Side

People were intrigued by Anning's discoveries of both ichthyosaurs and plesiosaurs. They inspired fellow fossil collector Thomas Hawkins to write his *Book of the Great Sea Dragons*, published in 1840. Hawkins believed that these "monsters," which inhabited Earth before humans, had lived in a sweltering, sunless world and were the work of the Devil.

SUPERHERO
FACT

People like Thomas Hawkins imagined the distant past to be a violent place full of monsters constantly battling each other.

In 1833, Anning was visited by the Reverend Henry Rawlins and his six-year-old son, Frank. Like most people of the time, Rawlins believed that God created the world in six days. Anning described to young Frank how she had found fossils at different levels in the cliffs, indicating that the creatures had been created and had lived at different times. According to Frank's later writings about the visit, his father refused to discuss the matter with him afterward.

Anning tried to reconcile her discoveries with her strong religious faith and continued to believe in God throughout her life. She came to accept that evolution and change were part of the divine plan.

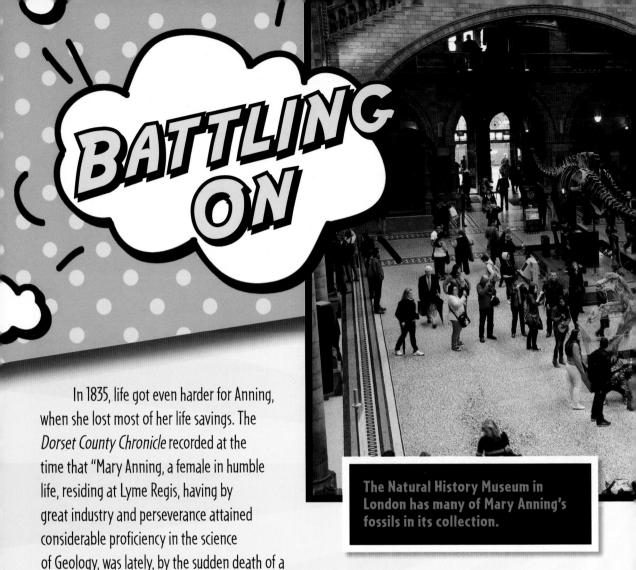

BATTLING ON

The Natural History Museum in London has many of Mary Anning's fossils in its collection.

In 1835, life got even harder for Anning, when she lost most of her life savings. The *Dorset County Chronicle* recorded at the time that "Mary Anning, a female in humble life, residing at Lyme Regis, having by great industry and perseverance attained considerable proficiency in the science of Geology, was lately, by the sudden death of a gentleman to whom she had entrusted ... a small property of about £200 (around $25,000 today), the fruits of her savings ... reduced to straitened circumstances, while her health was impaired from the hardships which she had exposed herself, and the distress of mind consequent on her loss."

Anning's friend William Buckland persuaded the recently formed British Association for the Advancement of Science to award her an annual payment of £25 (over $3,000 today), in recognition of her invaluable contributions to the science of geology. Some thought she should have had much more. The London publisher John Murray called it a "pitiable pension."

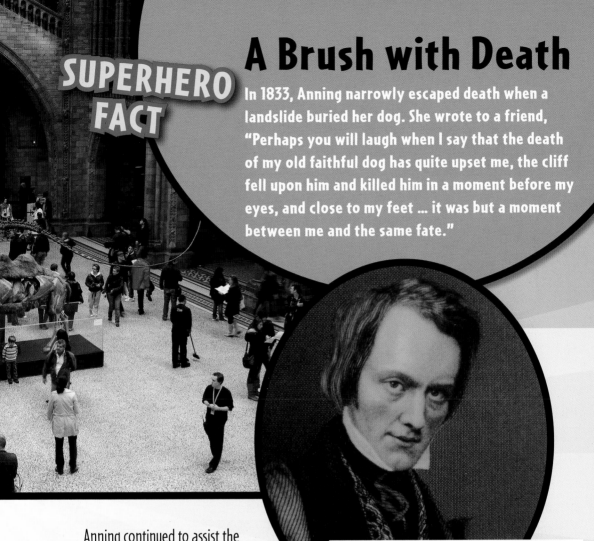

A Brush with Death

In 1833, Anning narrowly escaped death when a landslide buried her dog. She wrote to a friend, "Perhaps you will laugh when I say that the death of my old faithful dog has quite upset me, the cliff fell upon him and killed him in a moment before my eyes, and close to my feet ... it was but a moment between me and the same fate."

Richard Owen was a skilled researcher—but he was not popular with many of his fellow scientists.

Anning continued to assist the scientists who came to visit Lyme Regis in search of fossils. Thomas Hawkins was one, and she helped him hunt for ichthyosaur fossils. She was well aware, though, of his tendency to exaggerate his findings. Anning wrote, "He makes things as he imagines they ought to be; and not as they are really found . . . ."

In 1839, Anning led William Buckland, William Conybeare, and Richard Owen on a fossil-collecting expedition. Owen was a talented naturalist and skilled at interpreting fossils. He came up with the name "dinosaur" and was the driving force behind the setting up of the London Natural History Museum.

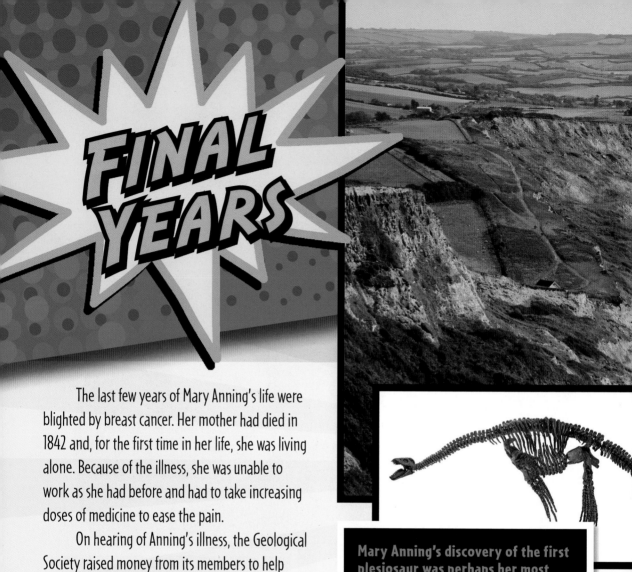

FINAL YEARS

The last few years of Mary Anning's life were blighted by breast cancer. Her mother had died in 1842 and, for the first time in her life, she was living alone. Because of the illness, she was unable to work as she had before and had to take increasing doses of medicine to ease the pain.

On hearing of Anning's illness, the Geological Society raised money from its members to help meet the cost of her treatment and her living expenses. It was proof that the science community held her in high regard, even if she was denied the recognition she deserved—as she well knew. In a letter to a woman in London, Anning had written, "The world has used me so unkindly, I fear it has made me suspicious of everyone."

According to the celebrated English writer and social critic Charles Dickens, the people of Lyme Regis were not very sympathetic to her misfortune. Rather than show sadness for the illness that was killing her, some accused Anning of turning to drink and drugs. After her death, there were also

Mary Anning's discovery of the first plesiosaur was perhaps her most important scientific contribution.

Exceptional Labors and Talents

Henry De La Beche, President of the Geological Society from 1847 to 1849, told a Society meeting that Anning, "... though not placed among even the easier classes of society, but one who had to earn her daily bread by her labor, yet contributed by her talents and untiring researches in no small degree to our knowledge [of ichthyosaurs and plesiosaurs]."

STAR CONTRIBUTION

The coast around Lyme Regis still draws visitors hopeful of making a spectacular fossil find.

those who complained about the lack of money coming to the town, as there were fewer important visitors.

Mary Anning died on March 9, 1847, at age 47. She had spent her entire life in Lyme Regis, leaving it only once for a short trip to London. Her brother Joseph, who had become the churchwarden in 1846, was buried beside her in the churchyard in 1849.

Members of the Geological Society contributed to a stained-glass window in her local church in her memory. It was unveiled in 1850. The inscription beneath the window says, "This window is sacred to the memory of Mary Anning of this parish . . . in commemoration of her usefulness in furthering the science of geology, as also of her benevolence of heart and integrity of life."

FAME AT LAST!

Charles Darwin built on the work of Mary Anning and the fossil hunters in his great theory of evolution by natural selection.

Boom!

Mary Anning's contributions to geology had a major impact at a time when few people understood the nature of our Earth and its true age. The spectacular fossils she brought to light forced scientists to look at different explanations for how the natural world had come to be as it is. William Buckland, William Conybeare, and many other scientists–though they often neglected to acknowledge her contribution–built their achievements on the back of her discoveries.

By the time of her death, geology had become well established as a scientific discipline. The way was open for people like Charles Lyell to suggest that the world was hundreds of millions of years old. Geologists began to date rock layers by the types of fossils that were found in them. Mary Anning's discoveries must have been invaluable in helping them to do this.

One of Anning's earliest customers at the Fossil Depot was Adam Sedgwick, another founder of

SUPERHERO FACT

Lost Legacy

Anning was an unsung hero of science. So many of her findings were sold to collectors and museums, without her ever receiving credit for them, that we may never know just how much she actually discovered.

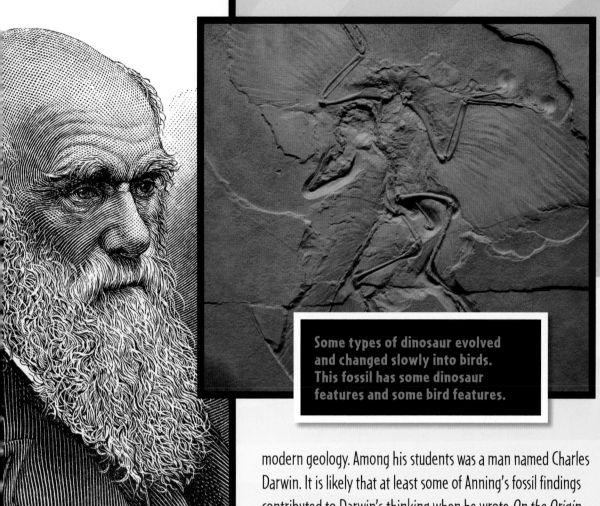

Some types of dinosaur evolved and changed slowly into birds. This fossil has some dinosaur features and some bird features.

modern geology. Among his students was a man named Charles Darwin. It is likely that at least some of Anning's fossil findings contributed to Darwin's thinking when he wrote *On the Origin of Species*—his great theory of evolution by natural selection.

In 1865, Charles Dickens applauded Mary Anning's struggle and achievements. He wrote, "The carpenter's daughter has won a name for herself, and has deserved to win it."

In recent years, Anning's contribution has also been more fully acknowledged in the scientific world. Scientist Stephen Jay Gould, writing in 1992, said that Anning was "probably the most important unsung collecting force in the history of paleontology." In 2010, she was recognized by the British Royal Society as one of the ten most influential women scientists in British history. On May 21, 2014, the 215th anniversary of Mary Anning's birthday, the Google search engine produced its own tribute—a "doodle" for its webpage that featured an illustration of her collecting fossils.

Glossary

ammonites an extinct group of ocean-living animals with spiral shells that were common during the Jurassic Period

anatomist someone who is an expert in anatomy, the branch of science concerned with the body structure of living things

belemnites an extinct group of ocean-living animals, common during the Jurassic Period, that were similar in appearance to today's squid and had internal cone-shaped shells, which formed fossils

breakwater a barrier built out into the sea to protect the ships in a harbor

Congregationalist a part of a late sixteenth- and seventeenth-century English Christian movement, where each congregation determined its own affairs, without the authority of figures such as bishops

coprolites fossilized feces, or dung

cycads plants of a type common during the Jurassic Period and similar in appearance to a palm

dinosaurs members of a large group of extinct reptiles that lived from about 250 million to 65 million years ago

dissected something cut up in order to study its internal parts

Dissenters English Protestants, including the Congregationalists, who disagreed with the Anglican Church

duck-billed platypus a type of mammal found in Australia, with a snout that resembles a duck's bill—one of very few mammals to lay eggs rather that give birth to live young

erosion the wearing away of rock and other surface material by wind, rain, ice, or other natural forces

extinction the disappearance of a species from Earth, when the last members of that species die

fossil the remains of a living thing from long ago that have been preserved by being turned into rock

geology the branch of science concerned with the study of Earth, what it is made of, and how it was formed

ginkgoes trees that first appeared during the Jurassic Period around 200 million years ago—and still exist today

ice age a time during the past when temperatures were much lower, and great areas of Earth's surface were covered in thick sheets of ice

Jurassic Period period of Earth's history from around 200 million to 145 million years ago, when dinosaurs, plesiosaurs, ichthyosaurs, and pterosaurs were the major forms of life

landslides sudden movements of rock or earth down the slope of a mountain or cliff

mammals warm-blooded animals, usually covered in hair or fur—the females produce milk to feed their young

paleontology the branch of science concerned with life in the distant past, usually involving the study of fossils and other remains

predators animals that hunt other animals for food

reptiles cold-blooded, scaly-skinned animals, such as lizards, snakes, crocodiles, and turtles

salamander a type of creature, similar to a newt, that can live on land or water

species a group of living things, whose members are very similar to each other

tuberculosis an infectious disease that affects the lungs

vertebrae the small bones that link together to form the backbone

World Heritage Site a special place, listed by the United Nations Educational, Scientific, and Cultural Organization (UNESCO) for its outstanding physical or cultural importance

For More Information

Books

Gray, Susan Heinrichs. *Paleontology: The Study of Prehistoric Life* (True Books: Earth Science). New York, NY: Scholastic, 2012.

Keller, Rebecca. *Focus on Elementary Geology*. Albuquerque, NM: Gravitas Publications, 2013.

Loxton, Daniel. *Evolution: How We and All Living Things Came to Be*. Toronto, Canada: Kids Can Press, 2010.

Walker, Sally. *Figuring Out Fossils* (Searchlight Books: Do You Dig Earth Science?). Minneapolis, MN: Lerner Classroom, 2013.

Websites

Dig into a database of almost 1,000 fossils from the Jurassic Coast where Mary Anning made her discoveries, at:
http://jurassiccoast.org/fossilfinder

Find out more about earth science from this NASA (National Aeronatics and Space Administration) website, specially designed to intrigue young minds, at:
http://kids.earth.nasa.gov

Explore the history of life on Earth through a series of interactive modules at:
www.ucmp.berkeley.edu/education/explotime.html

Index